2.00

TREASURY OF STORIES AND VERSE

Originally published as:

Hilda Boswell's Treasury of Poetry © William Collins Sons and Co. Ltd. 1968

Hilda Boswell's Treasury of Children's Stories © William Collins Sons and Co. Ltd. 1971

Hilda Boswell's Treasury of Nursery Rhymes © William Collins Sons and Co. Ltd. 1962

This arrangement copyright © William Collins Sons and Co. Ltd. 1989

This edition published in 1989 by Gallery Books,
an imprint of W.H. Smith Publishers Inc.,
112 Madison Avenue, New York 10016

Gallery Books are available for bulk purchase for sales
promotions and premium use. For details write or telephone
the Manager of Special Sales, W.H. Smith Publishers, Inc.,
112 Madison Avenue, New York, New York 10016. (212) 532-6600

Printed in Italy

ISBN 0 8317 4474 X

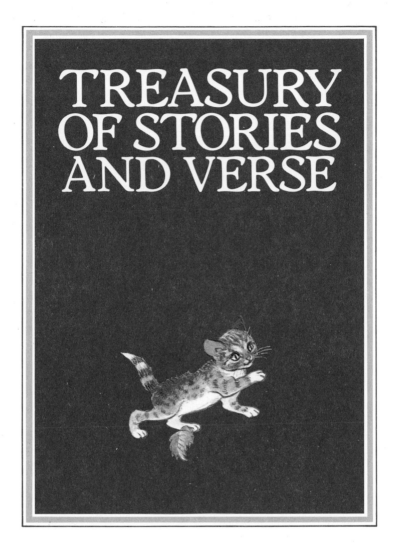

TREASURY OF STORIES AND VERSE

GALLERY BOOKS
An Imprint of W. H. Smith Publishers Inc.
112 Madison Avenue
New York City 10016

CONTENTS

Jack and Jill

Jack and Jill went up the hill
  To fetch a pail of water;
Jack fell down and broke his crown,
  And Jill came tumbling after.

Up Jack got, and home did trot,
  As fast as he could caper;
He went to bed and plastered his head
  With vinegar and brown paper.

Sing a Song of Sixpence

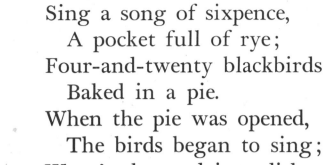

Sing a song of sixpence,
A pocket full of rye;
Four-and-twenty blackbirds
Baked in a pie.
When the pie was opened,
The birds began to sing;
Wasn't that a dainty dish
To set before the King?

The King was in the Counting-house,
Counting out his money;
The Queen was in the parlour,
Eating bread and honey.
The maid was in the garden,
Hanging out the clothes;
When down came a blackbird,
And pecked off her nose.

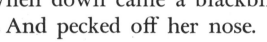

The Owl and the Pussy-Cat

The owl and the pussy-cat went to sea
   In a beautiful pea-green boat.
They took some honey, and plenty of money
   Wrapped up in a five-pound note.
The owl looked up to the moon above,
   And sang to a small guitar,
" O lovely pussy! O pussy, my love !
What a lovely pussy you are, you are,
   What a lovely pussy you are! "

Pussy said to the owl, " You elegant fowl!
　　How wonderful sweet you sing!
O let us be married—too long we have tarried—
　　But what shall we do for a ring? "
They sailed away for a year and a day
　　To the land where the Bong-tree grows,
And there in a wood, a piggy-wig stood,
With a ring on the end of his nose, his nose,
　　With a ring on the end of his nose.

" Dear pig, are you willing to sell for one shilling
　　Your ring? "　Said the piggy, " I will. "
So they took it away, and were married next day
　　By the turkey who lives on the hill.
They dined upon mince and slices of quince,
　　Which they ate with a runcible spoon;
And hand in hand on the edge of the sand
They danced by the light of the moon, the moon,
　　They danced by the light of the moon.

9

FIRELIGHT

I LIKE to sit by the fire and stare
    At the curious things I can see in there ;
It's better than pictures in a picture book
To sit by the fire and look, and look.

I can't see the things that Anne can see
(Anne, she's seven, but I'm just three)
Faces, and rivers, and forests, and all—
(Anne's enormous, but I'm quite small).

11

But the fire makes a nice sort of creaky song ;
It popples, as if it were running along ;
It talks quite soft, and it means to say,
" I know a nice quiet game to play."

I don't want to jump, and I don't want to shout ;
Mummy says, "What are you thinking about ? "
But I'm not thinking ; I just like to sit
Quite still by the fire, and stare at it.

A WARBLER

IN the sedge a tiny song
Wells and trills the whole day long ;
In my heart another bird
Has its music heard.

As I watch and listen here,
Each to each pipes low and clear ;
But when one has ceased to sing,
Mine will still be echoing.

13

THERE WAS AN OLD MAN WITH A BEARD

There was an old man with a beard,
Who said, " It is just as I feared!—
Two Owls and a Hen, four Larks and a Wren,
Have all built their nests in my beard! "

LUCY'S ADVENTURE IN NARNIA

C. S. LEWIS

O NCE there were four children whose names were Peter, Susan, Edmund and Lucy. They were sent away from London during the war to the house of an old professor who lived in the heart of the country. It was the sort of house that you never seem to come to the end of, and it was full of unexpected places. One room was quite empty except for a big wardrobe.

"Nothing there!" said Peter as they explored the house. Lucy stayed behind because she thought it would be worth while trying the door of the wardrobe. To her surprise, it opened quite easily. She stepped inside among several long fur coats which were hanging there, for there was nothing she liked so much as the smell and feel of fur. Of course, she left the door open because she knew it was very foolish to shut oneself into any wardrobe. It was almost quite dark and she kept her arms stretched out in front of her so as not to bump her face into the back of the wardrobe.

"This must be a simply enormous wardrobe!" thought Lucy, going still further in. Then she noticed that there was something crunching under her feet. "I wonder is it moth-balls?" she thought, stooping down to feel it with her hands. But instead of feeling hard, smooth wood, she felt something soft and powdery and extremely cold. "This is very queer," she said.

Next moment she found that what was rubbing against her face and hands was no longer soft fur but something hard and rough and even prickly. "Why, it is just like branches of trees!" exclaimed Lucy. And then she saw that there was a light ahead of her; not a few inches away where the back of the wardrobe ought to have been, but a long way off. A moment later she found that she was standing in the middle of a wood at night-time with snow under her feet and snowflakes falling through the air.

15

Lucy felt a little frightened, but she felt very inquisitive and excited as well. She looked back over her shoulder and there, between the dark tree-trunks, she could still see the open doorway of the wardrobe. "I can always get back if anything goes wrong," thought Lucy.

In about ten minutes she reached the light and found it was a lamp-post. As she stood looking at it, wondering why there was a lamp-post in the middle of a wood, she heard a pitter patter of feet coming towards her. And soon after that a very strange person stepped out from among the trees. He was only a little taller than Lucy herself and he carried over his head an umbrella, white with snow. From the waist upwards he was like a man, but his legs were shaped like a goat's (the hair on them was glossy and black) and instead of feet he had goat's hoofs. He also had a tail, but Lucy did not notice this at first because it was neatly caught up over the arm that held the umbrella so as to keep it from trailing in the snow. He had a red woollen muffler round his neck and his skin was rather reddish too. He had a strange but pleasant little face, with a short pointed beard and curly hair, and out of the hair there stuck two horns, one on each side of his forehead. When he saw Lucy he gave a start of surprise.

"Goodness gracious me!" exclaimed the faun.

"Good evening," said Lucy. The faun made her a little bow.

"Good evening, good evening. Should I be right in thinking that you are a Daughter of Eve?"

"My name's Lucy," said she, not quite understanding him.

"But you are what they call a girl?" asked the faun.

"Of course I'm a girl," said Lucy.

"You are, in fact, human?"

"Of course I'm human," said Lucy.

"To be sure, to be sure," said the faun. "How stupid of me! But I've never seen a Son of Adam or a Daughter of Eve before. I am delighted. Allow me to introduce myself. My name is Tumnus. May I ask, O, Lucy Daughter of Eve, how you have come into Narnia?"

"Narnia?" said Lucy.

"This is the land of Narnia," said the faun. "Have you come from the wild woods of the west?"

"I—I got in through the wardrobe in the spare room," said Lucy.

"Ah!" said Mr. Tumnus, "if only I had worked harder at geography when I was a little faun, I should no doubt know all about those strange countries."

"But they aren't countries at all," said Lucy. "It's only just back there—at least—I'm not sure. It is summer there."

"Meanwhile," said Mr. Tumnus, "it is winter in Narnia, and has been for ever so long, and we shall both catch cold if we stand here talking in the snow. Daughter of Eve from the far land of Spare Oom where eternal summer reigns around the bright city of War Drobe, how would it be if you came and had tea with me?"

"Thank you very much, Mr. Tumnus," said Lucy. "But I was wondering whether I ought to be getting back."

"It's only just round the corner," said the faun, "and there'll be a roaring fire—and toast—and sardines—and cake."

"Well, it's very kind of you," said Lucy.

"If you will take my arm, Daughter of Eve," said Mr. Tumnus, "I shall be able to hold the umbrella over both of us."

And so Lucy found herself walking through the wood arm in arm with this strange creature as if they had known one another all their lives.

They had not gone far before they came to a place where the ground became rough. Mr. Tumnus turned suddenly aside as if he were going to walk straight into an unusually large rock, but at the last moment Lucy found he was leading her into the entrance of a cave. As soon as they were inside she found herself blinking in the light of a wood fire. Then Mr. Tumnus stooped and took a flaming piece of wood out of the fire with a neat little pair of tongs, and lit a lamp. "Now we shan't be long," he said, and immediately put a kettle on.

Lucy thought she had never been in a nicer place. It was a little dry, clean cave of reddish stone with a carpet on the floor and two little chairs and a table and a dresser and a mantelpiece over the fire and above that a picture of an old faun with a grey beard.

Mr. Tumnus set out the tea things. "Now, Daughter of Eve!" he said. And really it was a wonderful tea. There was a nice brown egg, lightly boiled, for each of them, and then sardines on toast, and then buttered toast, and then toast with honey, and then a sugar-topped cake. And when Lucy was tired of eating the faun began to talk. He had wonderful tales to tell of life in the forest. Then he took from its case on the dresser a strange little flute that looked as if it were made of straw, and began to play. And the tune he played made Lucy want to cry and laugh and dance and go to sleep all at the same time. It must have been hours later when she shook herself and said:

"Oh, Mr. Tumnus, I really must go home. I only meant to stay for a few minutes."

"It's no good *now*, you know," said the faun, laying down its flute and shaking its head at her very sorrowfully.

"No good?" said Lucy, jumping up. "What do you mean? I've got to go home at once. The others will be wondering what has happened to me." But a moment later she asked, "Mr. Tumnus! Whatever is the matter?" for the faun's brown eyes had filled with tears and then the tears began to trickle down its cheeks, and at last it covered its face with its hands and began to howl.

"Mr. Tumnus!" said Lucy in great distress. "Do tell me what is wrong." But the faun continued sobbing as if its heart would break. "Mr. Tumnus!" bawled Lucy in his ear. "Stop it at once! What on earth are you crying about?"

"Oh—oh—oh!" sobbed Mr. Tumnus, "I'm crying because I'm such a bad faun."

"I don't think you're a bad faun at all," said Lucy. "You are the nicest faun I've ever met."

"Oh—oh—you wouldn't say that if you knew," replied Mr. Tumnus between his sobs.

"But what have you done?" asked Lucy.

"Taken service under the White Witch. I'm in the pay of the White Witch. It is she that has got all Narnia under her thumb. It's she that makes it always winter. Always winter and never Christmas; think of that!"

"How awful!" said Lucy. "But what does she pay *you* for?"

"I'm a kidnapper for her, that's what I am," said Mr. Tumnus with a deep groan. "Look at me, Daughter of Eve. Would you believe that I'm the sort of faun to meet a poor innocent child in the wood, pretend to be friendly with it, and invite it home to my cave, all for the sake of lulling it asleep and then handing it over to the White Witch?"

"No," said Lucy. "I'm sure you wouldn't do anything of the sort."

"But I have," said the faun.

"Well," said Lucy slowly, "well, that was pretty bad. But you're so sorry for it that I'm sure you will never do it again."

"Daughter of Eve, don't you understand?" said the faun. "I'm doing it now."

"What do you mean?" cried Lucy, turning very white.

"You are the child," said Tumnus. "I had orders from the White Witch that if ever I saw a Son of Adam or a Daughter of Eve in the wood, I was to catch them and hand them over to her. And you are the first I ever met."

"Oh, but you won't, Mr. Tumnus," said Lucy. "You won't, will you?"

"If I don't," said he, beginning to cry again, "she's sure to find out. She'll turn me into stone and I shall be only a statue of a faun."

"I'm very sorry, Mr. Tumnus," said Lucy. "But please let me go home."

"Of course I will," said the faun. "I hadn't known what humans were like before I met you. We must go as quietly as we can. The whole wood is full of *her* spies."

The journey back was not at all like the journey to the faun's cave; they stole along as quickly as they could, without speaking a word, and Mr. Tumnus kept to the darkest places. Lucy was relieved when they reached the lamp-post again.

She looked very hard between the trees and could just see in the distance a patch of light that looked like daylight. "I can see the wardrobe door," she said.

"Farewell, Daughter of Eve," said the faun. "C-can you ever forgive me?"

"Why, of course I can," said Lucy. "And I do hope you won't get into dreadful trouble on my account," and she ran towards the far-off patch of daylight as quickly as her legs would carry her.

Presently, instead of rough branches brushing past her she felt coats, and instead of crunching snow under her feet she felt wooden boards, and all at once she found herself jumping out of the wardrobe into the same empty room from which the adventure had started. She shut the wardrobe door tightly behind her. She could hear the voices of the others in the passage.

"I'm here," she shouted. "I've come back. I'm all right!"

LAVENDER'S BLUE

Lavender's blue, diddle, diddle,
Lavender's green;
When I am king, diddle, diddle,
You shall be queen.

Call up your men, diddle, diddle,
Set them to work,
Some to the plough, diddle, diddle,
Some to the cart.

Some to make hay, diddle, diddle,
Some to thresh corn,
Whilst you and I, diddle, diddle,
Keep ourselves warm.

Old King Cole

Old King Cole was a merry old soul,
    And a merry old soul was he.
He called for his pipe, and he called for his bowl,
    And he called for his fiddlers three.

Now every fiddler had a fine fiddle,
    And a very fine fiddle had he.
Tweedle, tweedle, tweedle-dee went the fiddlers,
    Tweedle, tweedle-dee.
Oh, there's none so fair, as can compare
    With King Cole and his fiddlers three.

Ride a Cock-Horse

Ride a cock-horse to Banbury Cross,
  To see a fine lady upon a white horse.
With rings on her fingers and bells on her toes,
  She shall have music wherever she goes.

*T*here was a crooked man

There was a crooked man
    Who walked a crooked mile.
He found a crooked sixpence
    Upon a crooked stile.
He bought a crooked cat
    Who caught a crooked mouse.
And they all lived together
    In a little crooked house.

There was an old man on the Border

There was an old man on the Border,
Who lived in the utmost disorder;
He danced with the Cat, and made tea in his hat,
Which vexed all the folks on the Border.

THE WRAGGLE TAGGLE GYPSIES

THREE gypsies stood at the Castle gate,
 They sang so high, they sang so low,
The lady sate in her chamber late,
 Her heart it melted away as snow.

They sang so sweet, they sang so shrill,
That fast her tears began to flow.
And she laid down her silken gown,
Her golden rings and all her show.

She plucked off her high-heeled shoes,
A' made of Spanish leather, O!
She would in the street, with her bare, bare feet,
All out in the wind and weather, O!

It was late last night, when my lord came home,
Enquiring for his a-lady, O!
The servants said on every hand,
"She's gone with the wraggle taggle gypsies, O!

30

"O saddle to me my milk-white steed.
Go fetch me my pony, O!
That I may ride and seek my bride,
Who is gone with the wraggle taggle gypsies, O!"

O he rode high and he rode low,
He rode through woods and copses too.
Until he came to an open field,
And there he espied his a-lady, O!

"What makes you leave your house and land?
What makes you leave your money, O?
What makes you leave your new-wedded lord,
To go with the wraggle taggle gypsies, O? "

"What care I for my house and land ?
What care I for my money, O?
What care I for my new-wedded lord?
I'm off with the wraggle taggle gypsies, O!"

" Last night you slept on a goose-feather bed,
With the sheet turned down so bravely, O!
And to-night you'll sleep in a cold open field,
Along with the wraggle taggle gypsies, O! "

" What care I for a goose-feather bed,
With the sheet turned down so bravely, O?
For to-night I shall sleep in a cold open field,
Along with the wraggle taggle gypsies, O! "

A PIPER

A PIPER in the streets to-day
    Set up and tuned and started to play,
And away, away, away on the tide
Of his music we started; on every side
Doors and windows were opened wide,
And men left down their work and came,
And women with petticoats coloured like flame.
And little bare feet that were blue with cold
Went dancing back to the age of gold,
For all the world went gay, went gay,
For half an hour in the street to-day.

SUMMER MORNING

THE air around was trembling bright
And full of dancing specks of light,
While butterflies were dancing too
Between the shining green and blue.
I might not watch, I might not stay,
I ran along the meadow way.

The straggling brambles caught my feet.
The clover-field was, oh! so sweet ;
I heard a singing in the sky,
And busy things went buzzing by;
And how it came I cannot tell,
But all the hedges sang as well.

Along the clover-field I ran
To where the little wood began,
And there I understood at last
Why I had come so far, so fast—
On every leaf of every tree
A fairy sat and smiled at me !

THEY WENT TO SEA IN A SIEVE

THEY went to sea in a Sieve, they did,
  In a Sieve they went to sea ;
In spite of all their friends could say,
On a winter's morn, on a stormy day,
  In a Sieve they went to sea!
And when the Sieve turned round and round,
And everyone cried, " You'll all be drowned !"
They cried aloud, " Our Sieve ain't big,
But we don't care a button, we don't care a fig !
  In a Sieve we'll go to sea ! "
Far and few, far and few,
Are the lands where the Jumblies live ;
Their heads are green and their hands are blue,
  And they went to sea in a Sieve.

They sailed away in a Sieve, they did,
   In a Sieve they sailed so fast,
With only a beautiful pea-green veil
Tied with a riband, by way of a sail,
   To a small tobacco-pipe mast ;
And everyone said who saw them go,
" Oh, won't they be soon upset, you know !
For the sky is dark, and the voyage is long,
And, happen what may, it's extremely wrong
   In a Sieve to sail so fast ! "

The water it soon came in, it did,
    The water it soon came in ;
So to keep them dry they wrapped their feet
In a pinky paper all folded neat,
    And they fastened it down with a pin.
And they passed the night in a crockery jar,
And each of them said, " How wise we are !
Though the sky be dark, and the voyage be long,
Yet we never can think we were rash or wrong
    While round in our Sieve we spin ! "

And all night long they sailed away ;
    And when the sun went down
They whistled and warbled a moony song,
To the echoing sound of a coppery gong,
    In the shade of the mountains brown.
" O Timballo ! How happy we are
When we live in a Sieve and a crockery jar,
And all night long in the moonlight pale
We sail away in a pea-green veil
    In the shade of the mountains brown ! "

They sailed to the Western Sea, they did,
 To a land all covered with trees,
And they bought an Owl, and a useful Cart,
And a pound of Rice, and a Cranberry Tart,
 And a hive of Silvery Bees.
And they bought a Pig, and some green Jackdaws,
And a lovely Monkey with lollipop paws,
And forty bottles of Ring-Bo-Ree,
 And no end of Stilton Cheese.

And in twenty years they all came back,
    In twenty years or more,
And everyone said, " How tall they've grown !"
For they've been to the Lakes, and the Torrible Zone,
    And the hills of the Chankly Bore ! "

And they drank their health, and gave them a feast
Of dumplings made of beautiful yeast;
And everyone said, " If we only live,
We, too, will go to sea in a Sieve—
    To the hills of the Chankly Bore!"

Far and few, far and few,
    Are the lands where the Jumblies live ;
Their heads are green and their hands are blue,
    And they went to sea in a Sieve.

THE BUCKLE

I HAD a silver buckle,
  I sewed it on my shoe,
And 'neath a sprig of mistletoe
  I danced the evening through !

I had a bunch of cowslips,
  I hid them in a grot
In case the elves should come by night
  And me remember not.

I had a yellow riband,
    I tied it in my hair
That, walking in the garden,
    The birds might see it there.

I had a secret laughter,
    I laughed it near the wall :
Only the ivy and the wind
    May tell of it at all.

THE LAMB

LITTLE lamb who made thee?
   Dost thou know who made thee?
Gave thee life, and bade thee feed
By the stream and o'er the mead;
Gave thee clothing of delight,
Softest clothing, woolly, bright;
Gave thee such a tender voice,
Making all the vales rejoice?
      Little lamb, who made thee?
      Dost thou know who made thee?

Little lamb, I'll tell thee ;
Little lamb, I'll tell thee :
He is calléd by thy name,
For He calls Himself a lamb,
He is meek and He is mild,
He became a little child.
I a child, and thou a lamb,
We are calléd by His name.
Little lamb, God bless thee !
Little lamb, God bless thee !

THE REAL PRINCESS

HANS ANDERSEN

THERE was once a Prince who wished to marry a Princess; but, he said, she must be a *real* Princess. He travelled all over the world in hopes of finding such a lady; but there was always something wrong. Princesses he found in plenty; but whether they were real Princesses it was impossible for him to decide, for now one thing, now another, seemed to him not quite right about the ladies. At last he returned to his palace quite cast down, because he wished so much to have a real Princess for his wife.

One evening a fearful tempest arose. It thundered and lightened, and the rain poured down from the sky in torrents; besides, it was as dark as pitch. All at once there was heard a violent knocking at the door, and the old King, the Prince's father, went out himself to open it.

It was a Princess who was standing outside the door. What with the rain and the wind, she was in a sad condition. The water trickled down from her hair, and her clothes clung to her body. She said she was a real Princess.

"Ah, we shall soon see that!" thought the old Queen-mother. However, she said not a word of what she was going to do; but went quietly into the bedroom, took all the bed-clothes off the bed, and put three little peas on the bedstead. She then laid twenty mattresses one upon another over the three peas, and put twenty feather beds over the mattresses.

Upon this the princess was to pass the night.

51

The next morning she was asked how she had slept. "Oh, very badly indeed!" she replied. "I have scarcely closed my eyes the whole night through. I do not know what was in my bed, but I had something hard under me, and am all over black and blue. It has hurt me so much!"

Now it was plain that the lady must be a real Princess, since she had been able to feel the three little peas through the twenty mattresses and twenty feather beds. None but a real Princess could have had such a delicate sense of feeling.

The Prince accordingly made her his wife; being now convinced that he had found a real Princess. The three peas were, however, put into the cabinet of curiosities, where they are still to be seen, provided they are not lost.

Was not this a lady of real delicacy?

If all the world were apple-pie

If all the world were apple-pie,
And all the seas were ink,
If all the trees were bread and cheese,
What should we do for drink?

Hickety, pickety, my black hen

Hickety, pickety, my black hen,
She lays eggs for gentlemen;
Gentlemen come every day,
To see what my black hen doth lay.

There was a Young Lady of Bute

There was a young lady of Bute,
Who played on a silver-gilt flute;
   She played several jigs
      to her Uncle's white pigs,
   That amusing
      young lady
         of Bute.

Early to Bed

Early to bed and early to rise,
Makes a man healthy,
wealthy
and wise.

Doctor FOSTER

Doctor Foster went to Gloucester,
in a shower of rain;
He stepped in a puddle
right up to his middle,
And never
went
there
again.

THE ROAD TO DOVER

CHARLES DICKENS

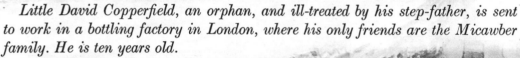

Little David Copperfield, an orphan, and ill-treated by his step-father, is sent to work in a bottling factory in London, where his only friends are the Micawber family. He is ten years old.

MR. and Mrs. Micawber and their family were going away from London, and a parting between us was near at hand. I had grown so accustomed to the Micawbers, and was so utterly friendless without them, that I felt my life was unendurable. It was in my walk home one night and the sleepless hours which followed when I lay in bed, that the thought first occurred to me to run away. To go, by some means or other, down into the country, to the only relation I had in the world, and tell my story to my aunt, Miss Betsey Trotwood.

As I did not even know where Miss Betsey lived, I wrote a letter to my old nurse, Peggotty, asking her if she remembered, and saying I had a particular occasion for half-a-guinea; and that if she could lend me that sum until I could repay it, I should be very much obliged to her, and would tell her afterwards what I had wanted it for.

Peggotty's answer soon arrived, and was, as usual, full of affection. She enclosed the half-guinea and told me that Miss Betsey lived near Dover.

I resolved to set out at the end of that week.

My box was still at my old lodging and I looked about me for some one who would help me to carry it to the booking-office. There was a long-legged young man with a very little empty donkey-cart, standing in the Blackfriars Road, whose eye I caught as I was going by. I asked whether he might or might not like a job.

"Wot job?" said the long-legged young man.

"To move a box," I answered.

"Wot box?" said the long-legged young man.

I told him mine, which was down that street there, and which I wanted him to take to the Dover coach-office for sixpence.

"Done with you for a tanner!" said the long-legged young man, and directly got upon his cart and rattled away at such a rate, that it was as much as I could do to keep pace with the donkey.

There was a defiant manner about this young man that I did not much like; as the bargain was made, however, I took him upstairs to the room I was leaving, and we brought the box down and put it on his cart; and he rattled away as if he, my box, the cart, and the donkey, were all equally mad; and I was quite out of breath with calling and running after him, when I caught him at the coach-office.

Being much flushed and excited, I tumbled my half-guinea out of my pocket; so I put it in my mouth for safety, and had just tied the direction-card on my box when I felt myself violently chucked under the chin by the long-legged young man, and saw my half-guinea fly out of my mouth into his hand.

"You give me my money back, if you please," said I, very much frightened; but he jumped into the cart, sat upon my box, and rattled away harder than ever.

I ran after him as fast as I could. "Give me my box and money, will you?" I cried, bursting into tears.

I narrowly escaped being run over, twenty times at least, in half a mile. At length, confused by fright and heat, I left the young man to go where he would with my box and money; and, panting and crying, but never stopping, faced about for Greenwich, which I had understood was on the Dover road.

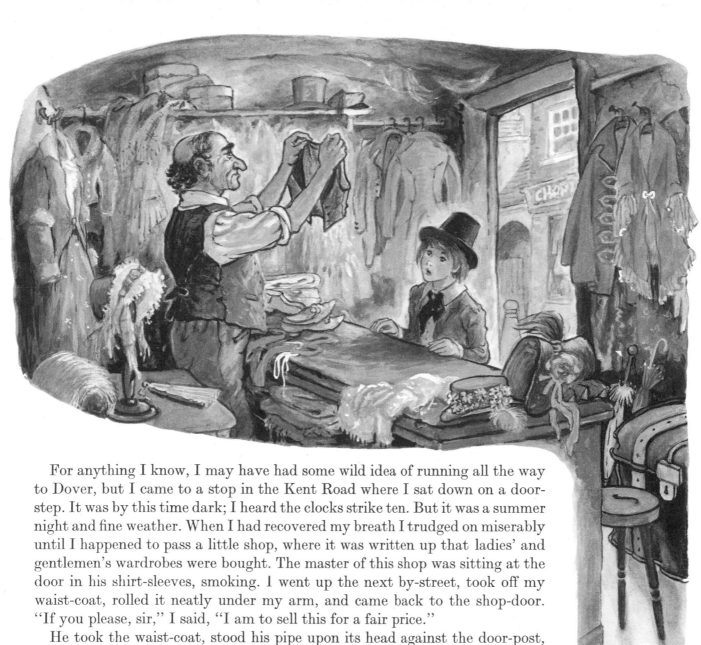

For anything I know, I may have had some wild idea of running all the way to Dover, but I came to a stop in the Kent Road where I sat down on a door-step. It was by this time dark; I heard the clocks strike ten. But it was a summer night and fine weather. When I had recovered my breath I trudged on miserably until I happened to pass a little shop, where it was written up that ladies' and gentlemen's wardrobes were bought. The master of this shop was sitting at the door in his shirt-sleeves, smoking. I went up the next by-street, took off my waist-coat, rolled it neatly under my arm, and came back to the shop-door. "If you please, sir," I said, "I am to sell this for a fair price."

He took the waist-coat, stood his pipe upon its head against the door-post, went into the shop, followed by me, spread the waist-coat on the counter, and looked at it there, held it up against the light and looked at it there.

"What do you call a price, now, for this here little weskit?" he said.

"Would eighteenpence be—?" I hinted.

"I should rob my family if I was to offer ninepence for it," he said and gave it me back.

I said I would take ninepence for it, if he pleased. Not without some grumbling, he gave ninepence. I buttoned my jacket and set off once again, with my ninepence in my pocket.

Never shall I forget the lonely sensation of first lying down without a roof above my head! I found a haystack and lay down by it and slept until the warm beams of the sun woke me. Then I crept away and struck into the long dusty track which I knew to be the Dover road. I heard the church-bells ringing, as I plodded on; and I passed a church or two where the congregation were inside, and the sound of singing came out into the sunshine. I felt quite wicked in my dirt and dust, and with my tangled hair.

I got, that Sunday, through three-and-twenty miles, and toiling into Chatham, crept, at last, upon a sort of grass-grown battery overhanging a lane. Here I lay down and slept soundly until morning.

Very stiff and sore of foot I was in the morning, and feeling that I could go but a very little way that day, I resolved to make the sale of my jacket its principal business. It was a likely place to sell a jacket in; for the dealers in second-hand clothes were numerous. At last I found one that I thought looked promising, at the corner of a dirty lane. Into this shop I went with a palpitating heart; which was not relieved when an ugly old man, with the lower part of his face all covered with a stubbly grey beard, rushed out of a dirty den behind it, and seized me by the hair of my head. He was a dreadful old man to look at, in a filthy flannel waistcoat, and smelling terribly of rum.

"Oh, what do you want?" he said. "Oh, my eyes and limbs, what do you want? Oh, my lungs and liver, what do you want? Oh, goroo, goroo!"

"I wanted to know," I said, trembling, "if you would buy a jacket."

"Oh, let's see the jacket!" cried the old man. "Oh, my heart on fire, show the jacket to us!"

With that he took his trembling hands, which were like the claws of a great bird, out of my hair.

"Oh, how much for the jacket?" cried the old man, after examining it. "Oh, goroo!—how much for the jacket?"

"Half-a-crown," I answered.

"Oh, my lungs and liver," cried the old man, "no! Oh, my eyes, no! Oh, my limbs, no! Eighteenpence. Goroo!"

"Well," said I, "I'll take eighteenpence."

"Oh, my liver!" cried the old man, throwing the jacket on a shelf. "Get out of the shop! Oh, my lungs, get out of the shop! Oh, my eyes and limbs—goroo!"

I never was so frightened in my life, before or since. So I went outside and sat down in the shade in a corner. And I sat there so many hours that the shade became sunlight, and the sunlight became shade again, and still I sat there waiting for the money. He made many attempts to induce me to consent to an exchange; at one time coming out with a fishing-rod, at another with a fiddle, at another with a cocked hat, at another with a flute. But I sat there in desperation; each time asking him, with tears in my eyes, for my money or my jacket. At last he began to pay me in halfpence at a time; and was full two hours getting by easy stages to a shilling.

"Oh, my eyes and limbs!" he then cried, "will you go for twopence more?"

"I can't," I said; "I shall be starved."

"Oh, my lungs and liver, will you go for threepence?"

"I would go for nothing, if I could," I said, "but I want the money badly."

"Oh, *go—roo*! Will you go for fourpence?"

I was so faint and weary that I closed with this offer; and taking the money out of his claw, went away more hungry and thirsty than I had ever been, a little before sunset. But at an expense of threepence I soon refreshed myself completely; and being in better spirits then, limped seven miles upon my road.

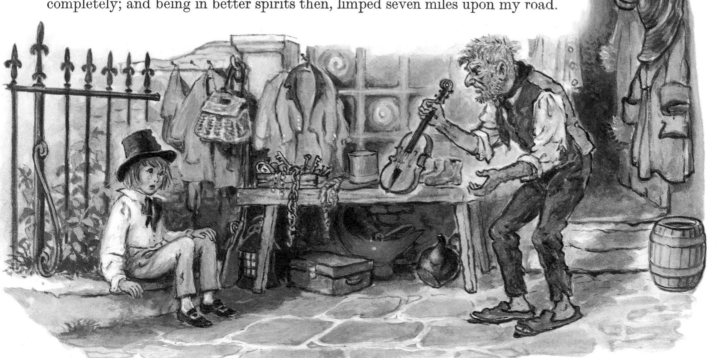

My bed at night was under another haystack, where I rested comfortably, after having washed my blistered feet in a stream. When I took the road again next morning, I found that it lay through hop-grounds and orchards. The orchards were ruddy with ripe apples, and in a few places the hop-pickers were already at work. I thought it all extremely beautiful, and made up my mind to sleep among the hops that night.

There were many trampers on the road next day. Some of them were most ferocious-looking ruffians, who stared at me as I went by. One young fellow, a tinker, roared to me in such a tremendous voice to come back, that I halted and looked round.

"Where are you going?" said the tinker, gripping my shirt with his blackened hand.

"I am going to Dover," I said.

"Where do you come from?" asked the tinker, giving his hand another turn in my shirt, to hold me more securely.

"I come from London," I said.

He made as though to strike me, then looked at me from head to foot.

"What do you mean," said the tinker, "by wearing my brother's silk handkercher? Give it over here!" And he had mine off my neck in a moment.

This adventure frightened me so, that, afterwards, when I saw any of these people coming, I turned back until I could find a hiding-place, where I remained until they had gone out of sight.

I came at last upon the bare, wide downs near Dover; and on the sixth day of my flight, there I stood with my ragged shoes, and my dusty, sunburnt, half-clothed figure, in the place so long desired.

I inquired about my aunt among the boatmen first; then the fly-drivers and the shopkeepers. I was sitting on the step of an empty shop at a street-corner, near the market-place, when a fly-driver, coming by with his carriage, dropped a horse-cloth. As I handed it up, I asked him if he could tell me where Miss Trotwood lived; though I had asked the question so often, that it almost died upon my lips.

"Old lady?" said he.

"Yes," I said, "rather."

"Pretty stiff in the back?" said he.

"Yes," I said. "I should think it very likely."

"Gruffish and comes down upon you sharp?"

My heart sank within me.

"Why then, I tell you what," said he. "If you go up there," pointing with his whip towards the heights, "and keep right on till you come to some houses facing the sea, I think you'll hear of her. My opinion is, she won't stand anything, so here's a penny for you."

I accepted the gift thankfully, and bought a loaf with it. I went in the direction my friend had indicated, and at length I saw a little shop and inquired if they could tell me where Miss Trotwood lived. A young woman, who was buying some rice, turned round quickly.

"My mistress?" she said. "What do you want with her, boy?"

"I want," I replied, "to speak to her, if you please."

My aunt's maid put her rice in a little basket and walked out of the shop; telling me that I could follow her. I followed the young woman, and we soon came to a very neat little cottage.

"This is Miss Trotwood's," said the young woman. "Now you know," and left me standing at the garden-gate.

I lifted up my eyes to the window above where I saw a pleasant-looking gentleman, who shut up one eye, nodded his head at me several times, laughed,

and went away. Then there came out of the house a lady with a handkerchief tied over her cap, and a pair of gardening gloves on her hands. I knew her immediately to be Miss Betsey, for she came stalking out of the house exactly as my poor mother had so often described her.

"Go away!" said Miss Betsey, shaking her head. "Go along! No boys here!"

With my heart at my lips, I went softly in and stood beside her as she stooped to dig up some little root.

"If you please, ma'am," I began.

She started and looked up.

"If you please, aunt."

"EH?" exclaimed Miss Betsey, in a tone of amazement.

"If you please, aunt, I am your nephew."

My aunt sat flat down on the garden-path. She stared at me until I began to cry; when she got up in a great hurry, collared me, and took me into the parlour. As I was quite unable to control my sobs, she put me on the sofa, exclaiming at intervals, "Mercy on us!"

After a time she rang the bell. "Janet," said my aunt when her servant came in. "Go upstairs, give my compliments to Mr. Dick, and say I wish to speak to him." The gentleman who had squinted at me from the upper window came in laughing.

"Mr. Dick," said my aunt, "don't be a fool."

The gentleman was serious immediately.

"Mr. Dick," said my aunt, "you have heard me mention David Copperfield."

"David Copperfield?" said Mr. Dick, who did not appear to me to remember much about it. "Oh, yes, to be sure. David, certainly."

"Well," said my aunt, "this is his boy—his son, and he has done a pretty piece of business. He has run away. Now, the question I put to you is, what shall I do with him?"

"What shall you do with him?" said Mr. Dick, feebly, scratching his head. "Oh! do with him?"

"Yes," said my aunt, with a grave look, and her forefinger held up. "Come! I want some very sound advice."

"Why, if I was you," said Mr. Dick, considering, "I should—I should wash him!"

"Janet," said my aunt, "Mr. Dick sets us all right. Heat the bath!"

The bath was a great comfort. For I began to feel pains in my limbs from lying out in the fields, and was now so tired that I could hardly keep myself awake for five minutes together. When I had bathed, they dressed me in a shirt and a pair of trousers belonging to Mr. Dick, and tied me up in two or three great shawls. What sort of bundle I looked like, I don't know, but I felt a very hot one. Feeling also very faint and drowsy, I soon lay down on the sofa again and fell asleep.

We dined soon after I awoke, off a roast fowl and a pudding; I sitting at table, not unlike a trussed bird myself, and moving my arms with considerable difficulty. All this time, I was deeply anxious to know what my aunt was going to do with me; but she took her dinner in silence, except when she fixed her eyes on me sitting opposite and said, "Mercy upon us!"

Afterwards, we sat at the window until dusk, when Janet set candles on the table, and pulled down the blinds.

"Now, Mr. Dick," said my aunt, with her grave look. "I am going to ask you another question. Look at this child."

"David's son?" said Mr. Dick, with a puzzled face.

"Exactly so," returned my aunt. "What would you do with him, now?"

"Do with David's son," said Mr. Dick. "Oh! Yes. Do with—I should put him to bed."

"Janet!" cried my aunt. "Mr. Dick sets us all right. If the bed is ready, we'll take him up to it."

The room was a pleasant one, at the top of the house, overlooking the sea, on which the moon was shining brilliantly. After I had said my prayers, and the candle had burnt out, I remember how I still sat looking at the moonlight on the water, as if I could hope to read my fortune in it. I remember how I turned my eyes away, and the feeling of gratitude which the sight of the white-curtained bed and the snow-white sheets inspired. I remember how I thought of all the solitary places under the night sky where I had slept, and how I prayed that I never might be houseless any more. I remember how I seemed to float down the moonlit glory of that track upon the sea, away into the world of dreams.

THE LION AND THE UNICORN

The lion and the unicorn,
Were fighting for the crown;
The lion beat the unicorn,
All round about the town.
Some gave them white bread
And some gave them brown;
Some gave them plum cake,
And sent them out of town.

Oranges and Lemons

" Oranges and lemons, "
Say the bells of
St. Clement's.

" You owe me five farthings, "
Say the bells of St. Martin's.

" When will you pay me? "
Say the bells of Old Bailey.
" When I grow rich, "
Say the bells of Shoreditch.

THE GARDEN YEAR

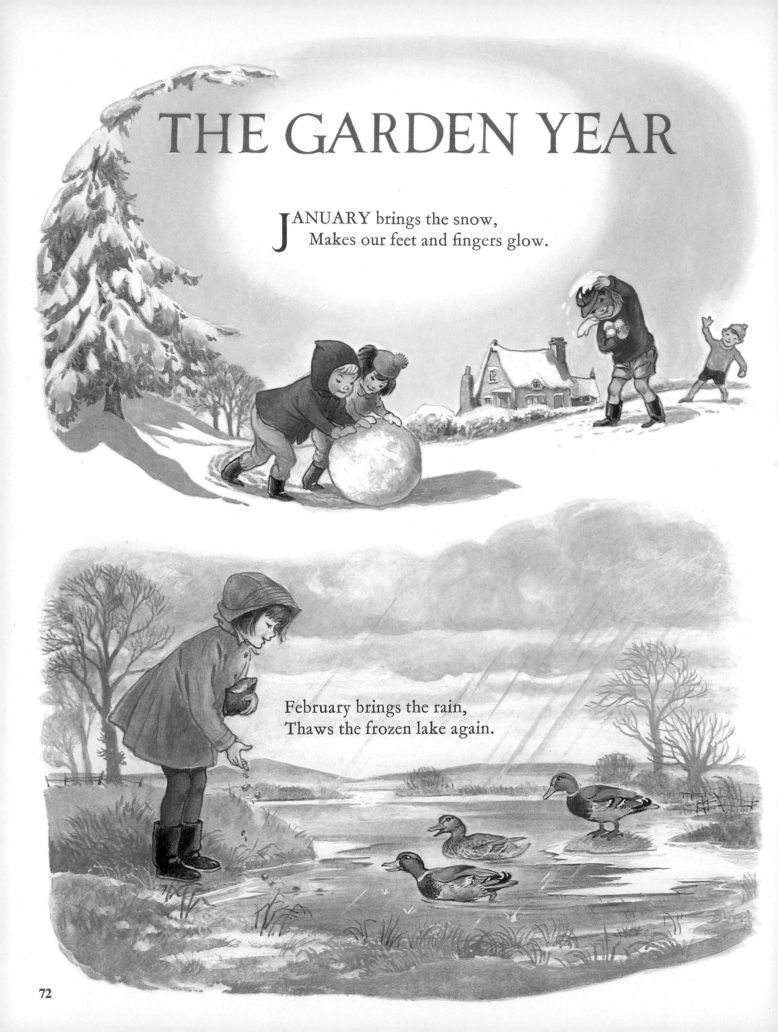

JANUARY brings the snow,
Makes our feet and fingers glow.

February brings the rain,
Thaws the frozen lake again.

March brings breezes, loud and shrill,
To stir the dancing daffodil.

April brings the primrose sweet,
Scatters daisies at our feet.

May brings flocks of pretty lambs
Skipping by their fleecy dams.

June brings tulips, lilies, roses,
Fills the children's hands with posies.

Hot July brings cooling showers,
Apricots, and gillyflowers.

August brings the sheaves of corn,
Then the harvest home is borne.

Warm September brings the fruit ;
Sportsmen then begin to shoot.

Fresh October brings the pheasant ;
Then to gather nuts is pleasant.

Dull November brings the blast ;
Then the leaves are whirling fast.

Chill December brings the sleet,
Blazing fire, and Christmas treat.

Two Little Kittens

Two little kittens, one stormy night,
Began to quarrel, and then to fight.

One had a mouse and the other had none,
And that's the way the quarrel began.

" I'll have that mouse," said the bigger cat.
" You'll have that mouse? We'll see about that! "

" I will have that mouse," said the older one;
" You shan't have the mouse," said the little one.

I told you before 'twas a stormy night,
When those two little kittens began to fight.

The old woman seized her sweeping broom,
And swept the two kittens right out of the room.

The ground was all covered with frost and snow,
And the two little kittens had nowhere to go.

So they lay them down on the mat at the door,
While the old woman finished sweeping the floor.

Then they crept in, as quiet as mice,
All wet with the snow, and as cold as ice.

For they found it much better, that stormy night,
To lie down and sleep, than to quarrel and fight.

Old Mother Hubbard

Old Mother Hubbard
Went to the cupboard,
    To get her poor Dog a bone;
But when she got there
    The cupboard was bare,
And so the poor Dog had none.

She went to the baker's
    To buy him some bread;
But when she came back
    The poor Dog was dead.

She went to the joiner's
    To buy him a coffin;
But when she came back,
    The poor Dog was laughing.

She took a clean dish
    To get him some tripe;
But when she came back,
    He was smoking a pipe.

She went to the alehouse
 To get him some beer;
But when she came back,
 The Dog sat in a chair.

She went to the tavern
 For white wine and red;
But when she came back,
 The Dog stood on his head.

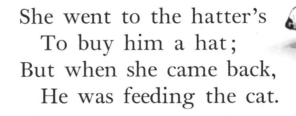

She went to the hatter's
 To buy him a hat;
But when she came back,
 He was feeding the cat.

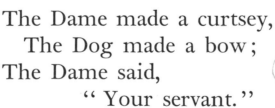

The Dame made a curtsey,
 The Dog made a bow;
The Dame said,
  " Your servant."
The Dog said,
  " Bow-wow!"

Ba-a, Ba-a, black sheep

Baa, Baa, black sheep, have you any wool?
Yes, sir, yes, sir, three bags full:
One for my master and one for my dame,
And one for the little boy
　　　　　　　　that lives
　　　　　　　　　　down
　　　　　　　　　　　the
　　　　　　　　　　　lane.

Simple Simon

Simple Simon met a pie-man
   Going to the fair;
Said Simple Simon to the pie-man:
   " Let me taste your ware."
Said the pie-man to Simple Simon:
   " Show me first your penny."
Said Simple Simon to the pie-man:
   " Sir, I haven't any."

WYNKEN, BLYNKEN AND NOD

WYNKEN, Blynken, and Nod one night
    Sailed off in a wooden shoe,
Sailed on a river of crystal light
    Into a sea of dew.
" Where are you going, and what do you wish ? "
    The old Moon asked the three.
" We have come to fish for the herring fish
    That live in this beautiful sea ;
Nets of silver and gold have we,"
        Said Wynken,
        Blynken, and Nod.

The old Moon laughed and sang a song
  As they rocked in the wooden shoe ;
And the wind that sped them all night long
  Ruffled the waves of dew ;
The little stars were the herring fish
  That lived in that beautiful sea.
" Now cast your nets wherever you wish,
  But never afeared are we ! "
So cried the stars to the fishermen three,
    Wynken,
      Blynken, and Nod.

All night long their nets they threw
   For the fish in the twinkling foam,
Then down from the sky came the wooden shoe,
   Bringing the fishermen home ;
'Twas all so pretty a sail, it seemed
   As if it could not be ;
And some folk thought 'twas a dream they'd
     dreamed
   Of sailing that beautiful sea ;
But I shall name you the fishermen three,
   Wynken,
     Blynken, and Nod.

Wynken and Blynken are two little eyes,
    And Nod is a little head ;
And the wooden shoe that sailed the skies
    Is a wee one's trundle-bed.
So shut your eyes while Mother sings
    Of wonderful sights that be,
And you shall see the beautiful things
    As you rock in the misty sea
Where the old shoe rocked the fishermen three,
    Wynken,
        Blynken, and Nod.

MICE

I THINK mice
Are rather nice.

Their tails are long,
Their faces small,
They haven't any
Chins at all.

Their ears are pink,
Their teeth are white,
They run about
The house at night.

They nibble things
They shouldn't touch
And no one seems
To like them much.

But I think mice
Are nice.

SWEET AND LOW

SWEET and low, sweet and low,
   Wind of the western sea,
Low, low, breathe and blow,
   Wind of the western sea !
   Over the rolling waters go,
   Come from the dying moon, and blow,
     Blow him again to me ;
While my little one, while my pretty one sleeps.

Sleep and rest, sleep and rest,
   Father will come to thee soon ;
Rest, rest, on mother's breast,
   Father will come to thee soon ;
   Father will come to his babe in the nest,
   Silver sails all out of the west
   Under the silver moon ;
Sleep, my little one, sleep, my pretty one, sleep.

THING-UM-A-JIG

"JUST the place for a Snark!" the Bellman cried,
  As he landed his crew with care;
Supporting each man on the top of the tide
  By a finger entwined in his hair.

" Just the place for a Snark ! I have said it twice :
    That alone should encourage the crew.
Just the place for a Snark ! I have said it thrice :
    What I tell you three times is true."

The crew was complete : it included a Boots—
    A maker of Bonnets and Hoods—
A Barrister, brought to arrange their disputes—
    And a Broker to value their goods.

There was one who was famed for the number
  of things
  He forgot when he entered the ship:
His umbrella, his watch, all his jewels and rings,
  And the clothes he had bought for the trip.

He had forty-two boxes, all carefully packed,
  With his name painted clearly on each :
But, since he omitted to mention the fact,
  They were all left behind on the beach.

The loss of his clothes hardly mattered, because
    He had seven coats on when he came,
With three pair of boots—but the worst of it was,
    He had wholly forgotten his name.

He would answer to " Hi ! " or to any loud cry,
    Such as " Fry me ! " or " Fritter my wig ! "
To "What you-may-call-um! " or "What-was-his-
        name ! "
    But especially " Thing-um-a-jig ! "

While, for those who preferred a more forcible word,
   He had different names from these :
His intimate friends called him " Candle-ends,"
   And his enemies " Toasted-cheese."

" His form is ungainly—his intellect small—"
   (So the Bellman would often remark)
" But his courage is perfect ! And that, after all,
   Is the thing that one needs with a Snark."

JACK BE NIMBLE

Jack be nimble,
Jack be quick,
Jack jump over,
The candlestick.

Lady-bird Lady-bird

Lady-bird, Lady-bird, fly away home,
Your house is on fire,
   and your children all gone.
All but the youngest,
   and her name is Anne.
And she has crept under
   the dripping pan.

THE SPIDER
AND
THE FLY

"WILL you walk into my parlour?"
    said the Spider to the Fly;
'Tis the prettiest little parlour that ever you did spy;
The way into my parlour is up a winding stair,
And I have many curious things to show
    when you are there,"
" Oh, no, no," said the little Fly;
    " to ask me is in vain;
For who goes up your winding stair
    can ne'er come down again."

" I'm sure you must be weary, dear,
   with soaring up so high ;
Will you rest upon my little bed ? "
   said the Spider to the Fly.
" There are pretty curtains drawn around ;
   the sheets are fine and thin ;
And if you like to rest awhile,
   I'll snugly tuck you in ! "
" Oh, no, no," said the little Fly ; " for I've often
   heard it said,
They never wake again who sleep upon your bed! "

Said the cunning Spider to the Fly :
    " Dear friend, what can I do
To prove the warm affection
    I have *always* felt for you ?
I have within my pantry good store of all that's nice;
I'm sure you're very welcome—
    will you please to take a slice ? "
" Oh, no, no," said the little Fly ;
" kind sir, that cannot be ;
I've heard what's in your pantry,
    and I do not wish to see ! "

" Sweet creature ! " said the Spider,
    "you are witty and you're wise ;
How handsome are your gauzy wings,
    how brilliant are your eyes !
I have a little looking-glass
    upon my parlour shelf,
If you'll step in one moment, dear,
    you shall behold yourself."
" I thank you, gentle sir," she said,
    " for what you're pleased to say,
And bidding you good-morning now,
    I'll call another day. . . . "

SANTA CLAUS

HE comes in the night ! He comes in the night !
   He softly, silently comes ;
While the little brown heads on the pillows so white
Are dreaming of bugles and drums.
He cuts through the snow like a whip through the
   foam,
While the white flakes around whirl ;
Who tells him I know not, but he findeth the home
Of each good little boy and girl.

His sleigh it is long, and deep, and wide ;
It will carry a host of things,
While dozens of drums hang over the side,
With the sticks sticking under the strings.
And yet not the sound of a drum is heard,
Not a bugle blast is blown,
As he mounts to the chimney-top like a bird,
And drops to the earth like a stone.

The little red stockings he silently fills,
Till the red stockings will hold no more;
The bright little sleds for the great snow hills
Are quickly set down on the floor.
Then Santa Claus mounts to the roof like a bird,
And glides to his seat in the sleigh;
Not the sound of a bugle or drum is heard
As he noiselessly gallops away.

He rides to the East, and he rides to the West,
Of his goodies he touches not one ;
He eateth the crumbs of the Christmas feast
When the dear little folks are done.
Old Santa Claus doeth all he can ;
This beautiful mission is his ;
Then, children, be good to the little old man,
When you find who the little man is.

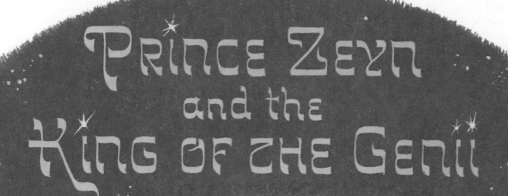

PRINCE ZEYN and the KING OF THE GENII

A story from The Arabian Nights.

THERE was once a King of Balsora who was very rich and good, and much loved by all the people whom he ruled. He had one son, whose name was Zeyn. Gathering together all the wise men in his country, he asked them to find out what sort of a boy the young Prince would be. So the wise men went out into the palace garden on a fine starlit night, and, looking up at the stars, said they could see wonderful things that would happen to Prince Zeyn.

"The stars say he will be very brave," said one wise man.

"They tell me that he will have strange adventures," said another.

"And he will live to be very old," added a third.

The young Prince grew up, and was taught everything that princes ought to know; but when he was still quite young, his father was taken very ill. Knowing that he was going to die, he sent for Prince Zeyn.

"You will soon be the king of this country," he said. "And I hope you will be a good one. Do not listen to those who are always praising you, and try to find out the real truth before you punish any one."

Prince Zeyn promised to remember his father's words, and afterwards the old king died.

At first Zeyn was not a good king. Being able to do whatever he liked, he spent most of his time in amusing himself and spending money. His mother, a very wise queen, reminded him of his father's words, and he began to feel sorry that he was not a better king, whom his people could love as they had loved his father.

But his money was all spent, and, not knowing where to get any more, he felt sad. One night he had a wonderful dream. He looked up and saw an old man standing beside his bed and smiling kindly down upon him.

"Oh, Zeyn," said the old man, "joy comes after sorrow, and happiness after sadness. The time of your riches has come. Tomorrow morning, take an axe, and dig in your father's room. There you will find a great treasure."

Now Zeyn did not believe this, but, feeling rather curious, he told the Queen his dream, and then, sending for an axe, shut himself up alone in his father's room. He dug up the pavement until he was quite tired, but at last his axe struck against a white stone, which he lifted eagerly.

To his surprise, he found a door fastened with a padlock. The axe soon broke this, and there, before the Prince, a marble staircase went down into the earth. Lighting a taper, Zeyn ran down, to find himself in a fine chamber with a crystal floor. All round it were shelves, and on the shelves ten big urns.

Zeyn took off the lid of the first urn, and found it full of gold. He then looked into the other urns, and behold, every one was full of gold. He took a handful to the Queen, who was greatly astonished, and went with him to the room where the treasure was hidden.

In one corner the Queen saw another little urn, and inside it was nothing but a key. "This must lead to another treasure," they said, and, looking round the room, found a lock in the middle of the wall, which the key just fitted. When it was turned, this door opened, and showed a large hall in which stood eight shining diamond statues upon eight large gold pedestals.

But there was one more pedestal which had no statue, and above it lay a piece of white satin on which Zeyn read these words written by his father: *My dear son, all these statues are for you. Go to Cairo and find an old slave of mine called Mobarec. He will show you a place where you may find a ninth statue more beautiful than all the rest.*

When he had read this, Zeyn set off to discover the ninth statue to fill the empty pedestal. Going to Cairo, he soon found the old slave Mobarec, who was now one of the richest men in the city.

"I am the son of the King of Balsora," said Zeyn.

"And how shall I know that you are speaking the truth?" said the old slave, looking straight into Zeyn's eyes.

"Because I can tell you my father had a secret room in which were ten urns full of gold and eight diamond statues. I have come to you to ask you where to find the ninth."

"You are indeed the young Prince!" cried Mobarec.

The next morning, Zeyn and Mobarec set out on their search for the ninth statue. The old man said that the Prince must be prepared to face many dangers, but as Zeyn was longing for adventures this did not frighten him.

After travelling for many days they came to some tall and waving palm trees, standing all around a lake of shining water. A silver moon looked through the trees and everything was very silent.

"You will now need all your courage," whispered Mobarec. "We are near the dreadful place where the ninth statue is guarded. We shall have to cross this water."

"But we have no boat," answered Zeyn.

"Wait a moment," said Mobarec, "and a fairy boat belonging to the King of the Genii will appear. But, however strange it looks, be very careful not to make a sound. If you speak, we shall all go to the bottom and be drowned."

Mobarec shaded his eyes and looked across the shining water. A little boat came into sight with an amber mast and a floating sail of blue satin. In a moment they had crossed the lake, the only sound being the soft rush of oars in the water.

"We may speak now," said Mobarec. "We are on a beautiful island belonging to the King of the Genii."

Very soon they came in front of an emerald castle with a golden gate, where several tall genii stood as guards. They were the fairies who lived on the island, and were tall and terrible to look at to those who did not understand them. But Mobarec did; so he took from under his robe two little square carpets, one for Zeyn, and one for himself. These were magic carpets, and those who sat on them were quite safe.

"The King of the Genii will be here soon now," said Mobarec. "If he is angry with us for coming, he will look like a monster; but if he is pleased, he will be very handsome."

There was a flash of lightning, a loud noise of thunder, and then all the island went dark. Suddenly a big, fine-looking man stood before them, and began to smile.

"Welcome, Prince Zeyn," he said. "I loved your father, and whenever he came to see me, I gave him a diamond statue for his very own. It was I whom you saw in your dreams, and I promised your father to give you the ninth statue, which is the most beautiful of all.

"But there is only one way to get it. You must search the world until you find a beautiful maiden who is not only clever but who has never in her life spoken an angry word or thought a wicked thought. When you have found her, bring her back here, to wait upon my Queen, and then I will give you the statue."

Zeyn promised to do all this, though he knew it would be a hard task; but he asked the King of the Genii how he should know the maiden.

"Here is a magic mirror," replied the King. "Only the right maiden will be able to see her face in this."

So Mobarec and Prince Zeyn went away into the world again to find a perfect maiden. They gathered together all the beautiful girls in Cairo, but not one of them could see her own face in the mirror. It grew dark and clouded whenever they looked into it. They next went to Baghdad, where they made friends with an old man named Muezin, who told them that he knew the most perfect maiden in the world.

She lived with her father, who had once been a great man at the King's court, but who now spent all his time teaching his daughter to be clever and good. Muezin took Prince Zeyn to see her, and when her father heard that he was the son of the King of Balsora, he was very pleased to see him, and at once allowed his daughter to look into the magic mirror.

The moment she did so, she saw her own lovely face in the shining glass, and every one standing round saw it too. Zeyn had found the perfect maiden that

110

he sought. Now there was only one way for him to get the maiden, and that was to marry her. Zeyn was quite ready to do this, for she was so good and beautiful that he already loved her. Indeed, he found it very hard to keep his promise, and take her back to the King of the Genii. He thought he would rather have the perfect maiden than the ninth statue.

The King of the magic island was very pleased with the maiden, and said she would be a beautiful slave for his Queen. Then he turned to Prince Zeyn and said, "I am quite satisfied with all you have done. Go home now, and when you reach your palace at Balsora, go down at once into the room where the eight diamond statues are. There you will find the ninth statue, standing on its pedestal."

Prince Zeyn went sadly home with Mobarec, leaving his lovely bride behind him. As soon as he reached the palace he told his mother all that had happened, and she was delighted to hear he would so soon have the ninth statue.

"Come, my son," she said, "let us both go down and look for the new treasure."

Together they went through the stone door, and down the marble staircase. They came to the diamond statues, and there Prince Zeyn stood still in surprise and delight. For the ninth statue was not made of diamonds or gold; it was the beautiful and perfect maiden whom he loved and whom he had been so sad to leave.

Hark, Hark, the Dogs do Bark

Hark, hark, the dogs do bark,
    The beggars are coming to town;
Some in rags, some in jags,
    And some in velvet gown.

Little Boy Blue

Little Boy Blue, come blow your horn,
　　The sheep's in the meadow,
The cow's in the corn.
　　But where is the boy who looks after the sheep?
He's under the haystack, fast asleep.

Pat-a-Cake, Pat-a-Cake

Pat-a-cake, pat-a-cake,
  baker's man,
Bake me a cake
  as fast as you can;
Pat it and prick it,
  and mark it with B,
Put it in the oven
  for Baby
  and
  me

Mary, Mary, quite contrary

Mary, Mary, quite contrary,
How does your garden grow?
With silver bells and cockle shells,
And pretty maids all in a row.

One, Two, buckle my shoe

One, Two, buckle my shoe,
  Three, Four, knock at the door,
Five, Six, pick up sticks,
  Seven, Eight, lay them straight,
Nine, Ten, the good fat hen.
  Eleven, Twelve, dig and delve,
Thirteen, Fourteen, maids a'courting,
  Fifteen, Sixteen, maids in the kitchen,
Seventeen, Eighteen, maids a'waiting,
  Nineteen, Twenty,
    my plate's
    empty.

The SNOW-CHILD

NATHANIEL HAWTHORNE

ONE afternoon of a cold winter's day, when the sun shone with chilly brightness after a long storm, two children asked leave of their mother to run out and play in the new-fallen snow. The elder child was a little girl called Violet, and her brother was known as Peony, on account of the ruddiness of his round little face. The children lived in a city, and had no wider play-place than a little garden in front of the house, divided by a white fence from the street, and with a pear-tree and two or three plum-trees overshadowing it, and some rose-bushes just in front of the parlour windows. The trees and shrubs, however, were now leafless, and their twigs were enveloped in the light snow.

"Yes, Violet. Yes, Peony," said their mother; "you may go out and play in the new snow."

Out went the two children, with a hop-skip-and-jump that carried them at once into the heart of a huge snowdrift. At last, when they had frosted one another all over with handfuls of snow, Violet was struck with a new idea.

"Peony," said she. "Let's make a figure out of snow—a little snow-girl—and it shall be our sister, and shall run about and play with us all winter. Won't it be nice?"

"Oh, yes!" cried Peony, as plainly as he could speak, for he was a very little boy. "That will be nice!"

"Yes," answered Violet; "Mamma shall see the new little girl. But she must not make her come into the warm parlour; for, you know, our little snow-sister will not like the warmth."

And at once the children began this great business of making a snow-child that should run about. Violet told Peony what to do, while she shaped out all the nicer parts of the snow-figure. It seemed, in fact, not so much to be made by the children, as to grow up under their hands.

"Oh, Violet, how beau-ti-ful she looks!" exclaimed Peony.

"Yes," said Violet. "I did not know, Peony, that we could make such a sweet little girl as this. Now bring me those light wreaths of snow from the lower branches of the pear-tree. I must have them to make our snow-sister's hair."

"Here they are!" answered the little boy. "Take care you do not break them."

"Now," said Violet in a very satisfied voice, "we must have some little shining bits of ice to make the brightness of her eyes."

"Let us call Mamma to look out," said Peony; and then he shouted loudly: "Mamma! Mamma! Mamma! ! ! Look out and see what a nice little girl we are making!"

The mother put down her work for an instant, and looked out of the window. Through the bright, blinding dazzle of the sun and the snow, she saw the two children at work. Indistinctly, she saw the snow-child, and thought to herself that never before was there a snow-figure so cleverly made. She sat down again to her work, and the children, too, kept busily at work in the garden.

"What a nice playmate she will be for us all winter long!" said Violet. "I hope Papa will not be afraid of her giving us a cold! Shan't you love her very much, Peony?"

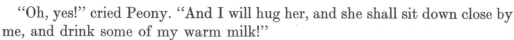

"Oh, yes!" cried Peony. "And I will hug her, and she shall sit down close by me, and drink some of my warm milk!"

"Oh, no, Peony!" answered Violet "That will not do at all. Warm milk will not be good for our little snow-sister. Little snow-people like her eat nothing but icicles."

There was a minute or two of silence; then, all of a sudden, Violet cried out:

"Look, Peony! A light has been shining on her cheek out of that rose-coloured cloud! And the colour does not go away! Isn't that beautiful?"

"Yes; it is beau-ti-ful," answered Peony. "Oh, Violet, look at her hair! It is all like gold!"

"Oh, yes," said Violet. "That colour, you know, comes from the golden clouds that we see up there in the sky."

Just then there came a breeze of the purest west wind, sweeping through the garden and rattling the parlour windows. It sounded so wintry cold, that the mother was about to tap on the window-pane with her thimbled finger to bring the two children in, when they both cried out to her.

"Mamma! Mamma! We have finished our little snow-sister, and she is running about the garden with us! Please look out and see."

The sun had now gone out of the sky and there was not the slightest gleam or dazzle, so that the mother could look all over the garden and see everything and everybody in it. Besides Violet and Peony, there was a small figure of a girl, dressed all in white, with rose-tinged cheeks and ringlets of golden hue, playing about the garden with the two children! The mother thought to herself that it must certainly be the daughter of one of the neighbours, and that, seeing Violet and Peony in the garden, the child had run across the street to play with them. So she went to the door, intending to invite the little runaway into her comfortable parlour. But, after opening the house door, she stood an instant on the threshold, hesitating. Indeed, she almost doubted whether it were a real child, after all, or only a light wreath of the new-fallen snow, blown hither and thither about the garden by the intensely cold west wind. Among all the children of the neighbourhood, the lady could remember no such face, with its pure white and delicate rose-colour. And as for her dress, which was entirely of white and fluttering in the breeze, it was such as no reasonable woman would put on a little girl when sending her out to play in the depth of winter. It made this kind and careful mother shiver only to look at those small feet, with nothing in the world on them except a very thin pair of white slippers. Nevertheless, the child seemed not to feel the cold but danced so lightly over the snow that the tips of her toes left hardly a print on its surface.

Once, in the course of their play, the strange child put herself between Violet and Peony, and took a hand of each; but Peony pulled away his little fist and began to rub it as if the fingers were tingling with cold; while Violet remarked that it was better not to take hold of hands. All this time the mother stood on the threshold, wondering how a little girl could look so much like a flying snowdrift, or how a snowdrift could look so very like a little girl.

She called Violet to her and whispered:

"Violet, my dear, what is this child's name? Does she live near us?"

"Why, Mamma," answered Violet, laughing, "this is our little snow-sister whom we have just been making!"

At this instant a flock of snow-birds came flitting through the air. They flew at once to the snow-child, fluttered eagerly about her head and alighted on her shoulders. She was as glad to see these little birds as they were to see her, and welcomed them by holding out both her hands.

"Violet," said her mother, greatly perplexed, "tell me the truth. Who is this little girl?"

"Mamma," answered Violet, looking into her mother's face, and surprised that she should need any further explanation, "I have told you truly who she is. It is our little snow-figure which Peony and I have been making."

While Mamma still hesitated what to think and what to do, the street-gate was thrown open and the father of Violet and Peony appeared, a fur cap drawn down over his ears and the thickest of gloves on his hands. His eyes brightened at the sight of his wife and children, although he could not help uttering a word or two of surprise at finding the whole family in the open air on so bleak a day, and after sunset too. He soon perceived the little white stranger, and the flock of snow-birds fluttering above her head.

"What little girl is this?" he inquired. "Surely her mother must be crazy to let her go out in such bitter weather with only that flimsy white dress and those thin slippers!"

"My dear," said his wife, "I know no more about the little thing than you do. Some neighbour's child, I suppose. Our Violet and Peony," she added, "insist that she is nothing but a snow-figure which they have been busy making in the garden almost all the afternoon."

As she said that, the mother glanced towards the spot where the children's snow-figure had been made. What was her surprise to see not the slightest trace of so much labour! No piled-up heap of snow! Only the prints of little footsteps around an empty space!

"This is very strange!" said she.

"What is strange?" asked Violet. "Father, do you not see how it is? This is our snow-figure which Peony and I have made because we wanted another playmate."

"Pooh, nonsense, child!" cried their father. "Do not tell me of making live figures out of snow. Come, wife; this little stranger must not stay out in the cold a moment longer. We will bring her into the parlour; and you shall give her a supper of warm bread and milk, and make her as comfortable as you can. Meanwhile I will inquire among the neighbours; or, if necessary, send the city-crier about the streets to give notice of a lost child."

"Father," cried Violet, putting herself before him, "it is true what I have been telling you! This is our little snow-girl, and she cannot live unless she breathes the cold west wind. Do not make her come into the hot room!"

"Nonsense, child, nonsense, nonsense!" cried the father. "Run into the house this moment! It is too late to play any longer. I must take care of this little girl immediately, or she will catch her death of cold!"

The little white creature fled backwards, shaking her head as if to say, "Please do not touch me!"

Some of the neighbours, seeing him from their windows, wondered what could possess the poor man to be running about his garden in pursuit of a snowdrift. At length, he chased the little stranger into a corner where she could not possibly escape him. His wife had been looking on, and, it being nearly twilight, was wonder-struck to observe how the snow-child gleamed and sparkled, and when driven into the corner, she positively glistened like a star!

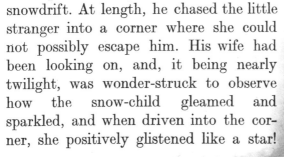

"Come, you odd little thing!" cried the children's father, seizing her by the hand, and with a smile, he led the snow-child towards the house. As she followed him, all the glow and sparkle went out of her figure and she looked as dull and drooping as a thaw.

Violet and Peony, their eyes full of tears, entreated him not to bring their snow-sister into the house.

"Not bring her in!" exclaimed the kind-hearted man. "Why she is so cold, already, that her hand has almost frozen mine, in spite of my thick gloves. Would you have her freeze to death?"

The little white figure was led—drooping more and more—out of the frosty air, and into the comfortable parlour. A stove, filled to the brim with intensely burning coal, was sending a bright gleam through the glass of its iron door. The parlour was hung with red curtains and covered with a red carpet, and looked just as warm as it felt.

The father placed the snow-child on the hearth-rug, right in front of the hissing and fuming stove.

"Now she will be comfortable!" he cried, rubbing his hands and looking about him with the pleasantest smile you ever saw.

Sad, sad and drooping, looked the little white maiden as she stood on the hearth-rug with the hot blast of the stove striking through her. Once she threw a glance towards the windows and caught a glimpse of the snow-covered roofs, and the stars glimmering frostily.

"Come, wife, give her some warm supper as soon as the milk boils," said the good man and turning the collar of his coat up over his ears, he went out of the house, and had barely reached the street-gate when he was recalled by the screams of Violet and Peony.

"Husband! Husband!" cried his wife. "There is no need of going for the child's parents."

"We told you so, Father!" screamed Violet and Peony, as he re-entered the parlour. "You *would* bring her in; and now our poor—dear—little snow-sister is thawed!"

In the utmost perplexity, he demanded an explanation of his wife. She could only reply, that, being brought to the parlour by the cries of Violet and Peony, she found no trace of the little white maiden, except a heap of snow, which, while she was gazing at it, melted quite away upon the hearth-rug.

"And there you see all that is left of it!" added she, pointing to a pool of water in front of the stove.

"Yes, Father," said Violet, looking reproachfully at him through her tears, "there is all that is left of our dear little snow-sister!"

"Naughty Father!" cried Peony.

But there is no teaching anything to sensible men like Violet and Peony's father. They know everything that has been, and everything that is,·and everything that possibly can be, and they will not recognise a miracle even if it come to pass under their very noses.

"Wife," said the children's father, after being silent for a time, "see what a quantity of snow the children have brought in on their feet! It has made quite a puddle here before the stove. Tell Dora to bring some towels and mop it up!"

Humpty Dumpty

Humpty Dumpty sat on a wall,
Humpty Dumpty had a great fall;
All the King's horses and all the King's men
Couldn't put Humpty Dumpty
together again.

Goosey, Goosey, Gander

Goosey, goosey gander,
    Where shall I wander?
Upstairs, downstairs,
    In my lady's chamber.
There I met an old man
    Who wouldn't say his prayers,
I took him by his left leg,
    And threw him down the stairs.

The Three Little Kittens

Three little kittens they lost their mittens,
And they began to cry,
  "Oh! Mother dear,
  We sadly fear,
  Our mittens we have lost!"
"What! lost your mittens,
  you naughty kittens!
Then you shall have no pie!"
  Miaow, miaow,
      miaow, miaow,
Miaow, miaow, miaow, miaow.

The three little kittens they found their mittens,
  And they began to cry,
    "Oh! Mother dear,
    See here, see here!
    Our mittens we have found!"
    "What! found your mittens, you little kittens
    Then you shall have some pie!"
        Purr, purr, purr, purr,
        Purr, purr, purr, purr.

MOUSE PIE

The three little kittens put on their mittens,
And soon ate up the pie;
"Oh! Mother dear,
We greatly fear
Our mittens we have soiled!"
"What! soiled your mittens,
you naughty kittens!"
Then they began to sigh:
Miaow, miaow, miaow, miaow,
Miaow, miaow, miaow,
miaow.

The three little kittens
they washed their mittens,
And hung them up to dry;
"Oh! Mother dear,
Look here, look here,
Our mittens we have washed!"
"What! washed your mittens, you darling kittens,
But I smell a rat close by!"
Hush! hush!—miaow, miaow,
Miaow, miaow, miaow, miaow.

Hey, Diddle, Diddle!

Hey, diddle, diddle, the cat and the fiddle,
The cow jumped over the moon.
The little dog laughed to see such sport,
And the dish ran away with the spoon.

Little Jack Horner

Little Jack Horner sat in a corner,
  Eating his Christmas pie!
He put in his thumb,
  And pulled out a plum,
And said, " What a good boy am I ! "

Little Polly Flinders

Little Polly Flinders
  Sat among the cinders,
Warming her pretty little toes;
  Her mother came and caught her,
And whipped her little daughter,
  For spoiling her nice new clothes.

Little Miss Muffet

Little Miss Muffet
　Sat on a tuffet,
Eating her curds and whey;
　There came a great spider
And sat down beside her,
　And frightened Miss Muffet away.

Rub-a-dub-dub

Rub-a-dub-dub,
　Three men in a tub,
And who do you think they be?

The butcher, the bakcr,
　The candlestick maker,
They all jumped out of a rotten potato,
　Turn 'em out, knaves all three!

A DAY ON THE ALM

JOHANNA SPYRI

EARLY in the morning, Heidi was awakened by a loud whistle. As she opened her eyes, a gleam of sunshine came through the little window on to her bed and shone on the hay nearby so that everything was bathed in golden light. Heidi looked puzzled and tried to think where she was. Then, from outside, she heard the grandfather's deep, quiet voice and she remembered that she was up on the Alm. She no longer lived with old Ursel who was almost stone deaf and always wanted to have Heidi by her side, so that sometimes the child had felt like a prisoner and would have liked to run away. So she was very glad when she awoke and found herself in her new home. She remembered all the exciting things she had seen the previous day and wondered what this new day had in store for her. Above all she looked forward to seeing the goats, Little Swan and Little Bear, again. Quickly she jumped out of bed and in a few minutes had dressed herself. Then she climbed down the steps and ran out to the front of the cottage. Peter, the goat-herd, was already there with his flock and the grandfather was leading out Little Swan and Little Bear to join them. Heidi ran forward to say good morning to him and the goats.

"How would you like to go with them to the pasture?" asked the grandfather.

Heidi was overjoyed. That was the thing she would like best of all.

"But first you must wash yourself or the sun, shining brightly up there, will laugh at you when he looks down and sees how dirty you are! See! This is where you wash." The grandfather pointed towards a big flat tub filled with water which stood in the sun before the cottage door. Heidi jumped towards it and splashed and scrubbed until she was perfectly clean. In the meantime, the grandfather went into the cottage, calling to Peter, "Come here, goat-general, and bring your rucksack!"

Amazed, Peter answered the call and laid down the rucksack in which he carried his meagre lunch.

"Open it!" ordered the old man, and then put in a big piece of bread and an equally big piece of cheese. Peter opened his round eyes very wide for this food was twice as much as he had for his own lunch.

"And now the little bowl has to go in," the old man continued. "At lunch-time you will milk for her two little bowlfuls, for she is going, too, and can stay with you until you come back in the evening. Take care she doesn't fall over the precipice!"

Now Heidi came running towards them. "Grandfather, the sun can't laugh at me now!" For fear of the sun's mockery she had rubbed her face, neck and arms so vigorously with the rough cloth which the grandfather had hung up beside the water-tub, that she was almost as red as a lobster.

The old man smiled. "No, he has no reason to laugh now," he agreed. "But do you know what happens when you come home in the evening? You go right into the tub like a fish because if you run like the goats your feet will get dirty. Now, off you go!"

Happily the children climbed up the Alm. The high winds during the night had blown away the last little cloud and now the sky was a vast expanse of deep blue out of which the sun shone and glittered on the green slopes. The little blue and yellow mountain flowers opened their cups and seemed to nod merrily at Heidi who romped everywhere. Enchanted by this sparkling, waving sea of flowers, she forgot all about Peter, even about the goats. All along the way she picked flowers until she had a big bunch which she wrapped in her pinafore, for she wanted to take them home.

Peter was quite dazed trying to look in every direction at once, for the goats, like Heidi, were jumping from one place to another. He had to whistle and shout and brandish his stick to bring the goats together again.

"Where are you now, Heidi?" came the boy's exasperated and rather angry cry.

"Here!" came the reply, but Peter could see no one. Heidi was sitting, hidden from view, behind a little hillock.

"Come here!" Peter called again. "You are not to go near the precipice the uncle said so!"

"Where is that?" asked Heidi, still not moving from her hiding-place.

"Up there! Right on the top the old eagle sits on the look-out for his prey." That did the trick.

At once Heidi jumped up and ran to Peter with her apronful of flowers.

"That is enough flower-picking for now," he said as they climbed up together, "if you are going to keep pace with me. And if you pick all the flowers to-day there will be none left for to-morrow."

Heidi was convinced. Moreover, her pinafore was so full that it could hardly hold another one. So she now walked quietly beside Peter. The pasture which

Peter usually chose and where he spent the day was situated at the foot of the high rocks. Bushes and fir trees covered the lower parts but nearer the summit the rocks rose bare and rugged towards the sky. On one side of the mountain, jagged clefts stretched far down and the grandfather had been right to warn Peter of the danger. When they had reached the pasture, Peter carefully put his rucksack into a little hollow in the ground, for the wind often blew with great violence across this part of the country and Peter did not want to see his precious possessions rolling down the mountainside. Then the boy, tired after the strenuous climb, stretched himself out at full length on the sunny pasture.

Heidi, by this time, had undone her pinafore and rolled it neatly round the flowers which she laid beside Peter's rucksack in the hollow. Then she sat down beside him and looked around. The valley lay far below, bathed in the sparkling morning sunshine. In front of Heidi a big, broad snowfield rose up to the dark blue sky and on the left stood a huge pile of rocks above which a bare rocky peak reached towards the sky, towering majestically above the child. Heidi sat motionless. A great silence was all around and only the delicate blue harebells and yellow cistus swayed softly in the gentle breeze, nodding joyfully on their slender little stems. Peter had fallen asleep and the goats were climbing high up amongst the bushes. Heidi had never been so happy. The golden sunlight, the fresh breezes and the delicate perfume of the flowers filled her with delight and she only wished that she might stay there for ever. She gazed so long at the mountains that it seemed to her that each had a face and that these mountain-faces were as familiar to her as old friends.

Suddenly Heidi heard a loud, harsh cry and when she looked up she saw, circling overhead, a huge bird, larger than she had ever seen before. His wings were outspread and he flew in a wide circle, coming back again and again and uttering loud, piercing shrieks above Heidi's head.

"Peter! Peter! Wake up!" cried Heidi, "Look! There is a big bird just above us!"

Peter got up and watched the bird, too, as it rose higher and higher and at last disappeared behind the grey rocks.

"Where has he gone to?" asked Heidi who had been watching the bird with keen interest.

"Home to his nest," replied Peter.

"Is his home up there? Oh, how nice to live so high up! How terribly he cries! Let's climb up there and see where his nest is!"

"Oh, no!" replied Peter emphatically. "Even the goats can't climb so high and the uncle said you were not to climb the rocks."

Suddenly Peter started to whistle and call loudly. Heidi could not think what this meant, but the goats apparently understood, for, one after another, they came springing down until they were all gathered together on the green slope. Some continued to nibble and others ran about, playfully pushing each other with their horns. Heidi jumped up and ran amongst them. While she played with the goats Peter fetched the rucksack and laid out the four pieces of bread on the ground, the big ones on Heidi's side and the small ones on his own. Then he took the little bowl, drew some milk into it from Little Swan and placed it in the centre. "Stop skipping now! It is time to eat," he said.

Heidi sat down. "Is the milk for me?" she asked.

"Yes," replied Peter, "and the two big pieces of bread and cheese are yours too, and when you have finished you get another bowlful from Little Swan."

Heidi began to drink her milk and as soon as she put down her empty bowl Peter filled it again. Then Heidi gave a big piece of her bread to Peter and all the cheese as well, saying, "You can have it all. I have had enough."

Peter gazed at her, speechless with surprise. Never in his life could he have given away as much as that. He hesitated a little, for he could not believe that Heidi meant it seriously. She held out the pieces, but as Peter still did not take them she laid the food on his knees. Peter had never before had such a satisfying lunch.

The animals had begun to climb up again towards the bushes; some skipping gaily over everything, others stopping to taste the tender herbs.

"Peter," Heidi said presently, "the prettiest of all are Little Swan and Little Bear."

"I know," Peter replied. "The uncle brushes and washes them, and gives them salt, and has the nicest shed."

Suddenly Peter jumped up and bounded after the goats. Heidi followed. Something must have happened and she simply could not stay behind. Peter forced his way through the middle of the herd to that side of the Alm where the bare and jagged rocks fell away steeply. Here, a heedless little goat might easily tumble down and break his legs. Peter had noticed inquisitive little Goldfinch jumping in that direction. The boy arrived just in time, for the little goat was just about to jump towards the edge of the precipice. Peter, lunging towards the goat fell down and only managed to seize one of its legs as he fell. Goldfinch gave an angry cry at finding herself caught and tried desperately to free herself. Peter could not get up and shouted for Heidi to help because he was afraid Goldfinch might wrench her leg. Heidi was already there and at once saw the danger. She quickly gathered some sweet-smelling plants from the ground and held them out towards Goldfinch, saying coaxingly, "Come along, Goldfinch, and be good! Look! You might fall down and hurt yourself."

The little goat turned quickly and ate the herbs from Heidi's outstretched hand. In the meantime Peter got to his feet again and held Goldfinch by the cord with which her little bell was fastened to her neck. Heidi grasped the goat in the same way at the other side of its head and together they led the truant back to the peacefully grazing flock. As soon as Peter got her back to safety, he raised his stick and started to give her a good beating. Goldfinch, however, knowing what was in store, timidly shrank back, and Heidi cried, "No, Peter! No! You mustn't beat her! Look how frightened she is!"

"She deserves it," Peter muttered, about to strike; but Heidi threw herself against his arm, crying indignantly, "Don't touch her! You will hurt her! Leave her alone!"

Peter turned surprised eyes on the fierce little girl and his stick dropped to his side. "All right, then, I'll let her off—if you give me some of your cheese to-morrow again," he bargained.

"You can have it all, to-morrow and every day. I don't want it," Heidi consented. "And I'll give you the bread, too, the same as to-day, but you must promise never to beat Goldfinch or Snowflake, or any of the goats."

"Suits me," said Peter, and that was as good as a promise. He let Goldfinch go and the little goat leapt joyously towards the herd.

So the day passed quickly and the sun began to sink behind the mountains. Heidi was sitting quietly on the ground, gazing at the cistus and the harebells which glistened in the evening sunshine; rocks and grass shimmered in a golden glow. Suddenly she jumped up and cried, "Peter! Peter! They are on fire! They are all on fire! All the mountains are burning! And the great snow mountain also, and the sky! Oh, look at the lovely fiery snow! Peter, get up and look! The fire is at the great bird's nest, too. Look at the rocks and the fir trees! Everything is on fire!"

"It is always like that," replied Peter with great unconcern, "but it is not real fire."

"What is it, then?" asked Heidi, gazing eagerly around. "What is it, Peter?"

"It just gets like that," Peter tried to explain.

"Oh, look, Peter!" cried Heidi again in great excitement. "Everything is turning a rosy pink colour. Look at the snow and the high rocks! What are their names, Peter?"

"Mountains don't have names," replied Peter.

"Oh, how beautiful! Crimson snow! Oh, now all the rocks are turning grey— now the colour is all gone. Now it is all over, Peter."

Heidi sat down, looking as distressed as if everything really had come to an end.

"To-morrow it will be the same," said Peter. "Get up now. We must go home."

"Will it be like this every day we are on the pasture?" asked Heidi insistently, as she walked down the Alm at Peter's side.

"Mostly," he replied.

Heidi was very happy. She had absorbed so many new impressions—had so many new things to think about that she was quite silent until they reached the hut and saw the grandfather sitting on the bench under the fir trees. Here he sat in the evenings, waiting for his goats.

Heidi ran up to him, followed by Little Swan and Little Bear, for the goats knew their master.

"Good night!" Peter called after Heidi, and then added, "Come again, to-morrow!" because he was very anxious for her to go with him.

Heidi raced towards the old man.

"Oh, Grandfather, it was wonderful!" she cried long before she reached him. "The fire on the snow and the rocks and the blue and yellow flowers, and look what I have brought for you!" Heidi unfolded her pinafore and all the flowers fell at the grandfather's feet. But what a sight the poor flowers were! Heidi did not recognise them. They were like withered grass and not a single little cup was open. "Grandfather, what is the matter with the flowers?" cried Heidi, quite alarmed. "They weren't like that before. What is wrong with them?"

"They would rather be out in the sun than tied up in a pinafore," explained the grandfather.

"Then I will never gather any more. But Grandfather, why did the eagle screech so?" Heidi asked.

"You had better have your bath now," said the grandfather, "and I shall

fetch some milk from the shed. Afterwards, when we are having our supper you can tell me about everything."

Later, when Heidi sat in her high chair, the little bowl of milk in front of her and the grandfather at her side, she again asked her question.

"Why did the great bird scream at us, Grandfather?"

"He screams in mockery of the people in the villages down in the valley where they sit gossiping together. He wants to say, 'If you would all mind your own business or climb up into the heights like me you would be much happier!'"

The grandfather spoke these words with such vehemence that Heidi seemed to hear again the croaking of the great bird.

"Why don't the mountains have names, Grandfather?" asked Heidi again.

"They have names," he answered, "and if you can describe one to me so that I can recognise it, then I will tell you its name."

Heidi tried to describe the rocky mountain with the two high peaks exactly as she had seen it. Presently the grandfather interrupted, "Yes, I know that one. Its name is Falknis. Did you notice any others?"

Then Heidi recalled the mountain with the large snowfield which looked at first as if it were on fire and then turned rose-coloured, then pale pink, and at last faded back to its own grey colour.

"I know that one, too," said the grandfather. "That is the Scesaplana. Did you like being on the pasture?"

Now Heidi told him everything: how wonderful it had been and particularly about the fire in the evening. Heidi wanted the grandfather to explain why this had happened, since Peter had been unable to do so.

"You see," the grandfather instructed her, "that's what the sun does when he says good night to the mountains. He throws his most beautiful rays over them so that they won't forget him before morning."

Heidi was delighted. She could hardly wait for the next day when she would again be allowed to go to the pasture, to watch how the sun said good night to the mountains. But first she had to go to bed, and how soundly she slept all night on her hay bed and dreamt of nothing but glistening mountains tinged with red, and Little Snowflake running happily about!

Pussy-cat, Pussy-cat

"Pussy-cat, pussy-cat,
   Where have you been?"
"I've been to London
   To visit the Queen."
"Pussy-cat, pussy-cat,
   What did you there?"
"I frightened a little mouse
   Under the chair."

Tom, Tom, the Piper's son

Tom, Tom, the Piper's son,
   Stole a pig, and away he run.
The pig was eat, and Tom was beat,
   And Tom went roaring down the street.

Hush-a-Bye, Baby.

Hush-a-bye, baby,
    on the tree-top,
When the wind blows
    the cradle will rock;
When the bough breaks
    the cradle will fall,
Down will come baby,
    cradle
        and all.

THE HOUSE THAT JACK BUILT

This is the house that Jack built.

This is the malt
That lay in the house
          that Jack built.

This is the rat
That ate the malt
That lay in the house that Jack built.

This is the cat
That killed the rat
That ate the malt
That lay in the house
          that Jack built.

This is the dog
That worried the cat
That killed the rat
That ate the malt
That lay in the house
      that Jack built.

This is the cow with the crumpled horn
That tossed the dog
That worried the cat
That killed the rat
That ate the malt
That lay in the house
      that Jack built.

This is the maiden all forlorn
   That milked the cow with
      the crumpled horn
   That tossed the dog
   That worried the cat
   That killed the rat
   That ate the malt
   That lay in the house
      that
      Jack
      built.

Three Blind Mice

Three blind mice, see how they run!
They all run after the farmer's wife,
Who cut off their tails
   with the carving-knife.
Did ever you see

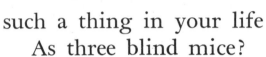

    such a thing in your life
    As three blind mice?

Handy-Pandy

Handy-pandy, Jack-a-dandy,
Loved plum cake and sugar-candy;
He bought some at a grocer's shop,
And out he came,
      hop,
        hop,
          hop.

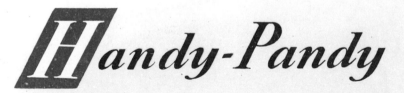

Mary had a little lamb

Mary had a little lamb,
   Its fleece was white as snow.
And everywhere that Mary went
   The lamb was sure to go.

It followed her to school one day,
   Which was against the rule;
It made the children laugh and play
   To see a lamb at school.

And so the teacher turned it out,
   But still it lingered near,
And waited patiently about
   Till Mary did appear.

"What makes the lamb love Mary so?"
   The eager children cry.
"Why, Mary loves the lamb, you know."
   And that's the reason why.

THIS LITTLE PIG

This little pig went to market,

This little pig
stayed
at home,

This little pig had roast beef,

This little pig had none,

And this little pig cried,
Wee, Wee, Wee, all the way home.

The Queen of Hearts

The Queen of Hearts,
    She made some tarts,
All on a summer's day;
    The Knave of Hearts,
He stole those tarts,
    And took them clean away.

The King of Hearts
    Called for those tarts,
And beat the Knave full score;
    The Knave of Hearts
Brought back those tarts,
    And vow'd he'd steal no more.

Little Bo-peep

Little Bo-peep has lost her sheep,
   And doesn't know where to find them,
Leave them alone, and they'll come home,
   Bringing their tails behind them.

Little Bo-peep fell fast asleep,
   And dreamt she heard them bleating;
When she awoke, 'twas all a joke,
   For they were still a-fleeting.

Then up she took her little crook,
   Determined for to find them;
She found them indeed,
   But it made her heart bleed,
For they'd left their tails behind them.

It happened one day,
      as Bo-peep did stray
Into a meadow hard by,
Then she espied their tails,
         side by side,
All hung on a tree to dry.

152

I had a little nut-tree

I had a little nut-tree,
    nothing would it bear,
But a silver nutmeg and a golden pear;
The King of Spain's daughter
    came to visit me,
        And all was because
        of my little
        nut-tree.

I saw a ship a-sailing

I saw a ship a-sailing,
        a-sailing on the sea;
And, oh! It was all laden
        with pretty things for thee!
There were comfits in the cabin
        and apples in the hold;
The sails were all of silk,
        and the masts were made of gold.
The four-and-twenty sailors
        that stood between the decks,
Were four-and-twenty white mice
        with chains about their necks.
The captain was a duck
        with a packet on his back;
And when the ship began to move,
        the captain said,
        " Quack! Quack!"

Come let's to bed

" Come let's to bed," says Sleepy Head,
" Tarry awhile," says Slow.
" Put on the pan," says Greedy Nan,
" We'll sup before we go."

Wee Willie Winkie

Wee Willie Winkie runs through the town,
Upstairs and downstairs, in his nightgown;
Rapping at the window, crying through the lock,
"Are the children in their beds?
For now it's eight o'clock."

BEDTIME

THE evening is coming,
   The sun sinks to rest ;
The rooks are all flying
   Straight home to the nest,
" Caw ! " says the rook, as he flies overhead,
" It's time little people were going to bed ! "

The flowers are closing ;
    The daisy's asleep,
The primrose is buried
    In slumber so deep.
Shut up for the night is the pimpernel red ;
It's time little people were going to bed !

The butterfly drowsy,
    Has folded its wing ;
The bees are returning,
    No more the birds sing.
Their labour is over, their nestlings are fed ;
It's time little people were going to bed !

Here comes the pony,
  His work is all done ;
Down through the meadow
  He takes a good run ;
Up go his heels, and down goes his head ;
It's time little people were going to bed !

Good night, little people,
  Good night and good night ;
Sweet dreams to your eyelids
  Till dawning of light ;
The evening has come, there's no more to be said,
It's time little people were going to bed !

Acknowledgements

For kind permission to include copyright material, the compiler and publishers of this book offer their thanks to the following:

The Literary Trustees of Walter de la Mare and The Society of Authors as their representative for "The Buckle" and "A Warbler" by Walter de la Mare. Messrs. F. Muller for "Firelight" from Six O'Clock And After by Irene and Aubrey de Selincourt. The Society of Authors as the literary representative of the Estate of the late Miss Rose Fyleman for "Summer Morning" and "Mice" by Rose Fyleman. Mrs Estella Starkey for "A Piper" by Seumas O'Sullivan.

Other poetry included in this collection was written by:

Edward Lear (They Went to Sea in a Sieve), William Blake (The Lamb), Sara Coleridge (The Garden Year), Eugene Field (Wynken, Blynken and Nod), Alfred, Lord Tennyson (Sweet and Low), Lewis Carroll (Thing-Um-A-Jig), Mary Howitt (The Spider and the Fly), Thomas Hood (Bedtime).